TreeTops *True* Stories

ANTARCTIC ADVENTURE

Crossing the Frozen Continent

Anna Perera

Illustrated by Trevor Parkin

OXFORD
UNIVERSITY PRESS

OXFORD

UNIVERSITY PRESS

Great Clarendon Street, Oxford OX2 6DP

Oxford University Press is a department of the University of Oxford.
It furthers the University's objective of excellence in research, scholarship,
and education by publishing worldwide in

Oxford New York

Auckland Bangkok Buenos Aires Cape Town Chennai
Dar es Salaam Delhi Hong Kong Istanbul Karachi Kolkata
Kuala Lumpur Madrid Melbourne Mexico City Mumbai Nairobi
São Paulo Shanghai Taipei Tokyo Toronto

Oxford is a registered trade mark of Oxford University Press
in the UK and in certain other countries

British Library Cataloguing in Publication Data

Data available

ISBN 0 19 919644 3

1 3 5 7 9 10 8 6 4 2

Mixed Pack (1 of 6 different titles): ISBN 0 19 919647 8
Class Pack (6 copies of 6 titles): ISBN 0 19 919646 X

Illustrated by Trevor Parkin c/o Linda Rogers Associates
Cover photo by Katz Pictures

Acknowledgements
p4 Gamble David/Sygma/Corbis UK Ltd.; p4/5 Corel; p5 Jones
Jon/Sygma/Corbis UK Ltd.; p6 Yann Arthus-Bertrand/Corbis UK
Ltd.; p8 Ranulph Fiennes/Royal Geographical Society; p12
Ranulph Fiennes/Royal Geographical Society; p16 John Cleare
Mountain Camera; p16 John Cleare Mountain Camera; p51
Ranulph Fiennes/Royal Geographical Society; p55 Ranulph
Fiennes/Royal Geographical Society; p57 Galen Rowell/
Corbis UK Ltd.; pp62/63 Corel.

Printed in China

Contents

Introduction

On the 9th of November 1992, a **ski-plane** dropped Sir Ranulph Fiennes and Dr Mike Stroud at the edge of Antarctica. It left them in the sweeping whiteness of the world's fifth largest continent, home to 90% of the world's ice.

The explorer, Sir Ranulph Fiennes

Dr Stroud, who accompanied
Sir Ranulph on a walk across Antarctica

This is the true, horrible tale of the first bid to cross Antarctica without help of any kind. No dogs. No rescue planes on standby. No food or equipment drops. Just two men, their overloaded sledges, and their desire to be first!

CHAPTER

1

Full to Bursting

The Antarctic landscape

Ever seen ice crack and drift out to sea?
Ever seen **crevasses** wider than houses
open up in front of you? Ever been
snow-blind? Antarctica's the wildest,
most dangerous place on earth *and* it's
the coldest. One wrong step, one
unlucky move – and it's over.

Ranulph and Mike's sledges were full to bursting. Everything they needed for the next three months was packed in tight. They hadn't had enough money to pay for all the things they needed. Important things like a rescue plane if they ran into trouble on the way. So if anything went wrong, well, you get the picture. There was no back-up.

If one of them got hurt, they would just have to give up and crawl home. Imagine the shame of that! They were raising money for charity and wanted to raise as much as possible. And, of course, they wanted to be the first to cross the Antarctic without any help.

Day 1

Ranulph Fiennes and Mike Stroud watched the ski-plane buzz away from them. When it disappeared from view they slowly fixed the sledge harnesses to

*Getting ready for the
hard slog ahead of them*

their waists and shoulders and stared
out at the nothingness all around them.
This was the moment of truth. Were the
sledges too heavy to pull? Would they
move at all? Until now they hadn't tried
them. It would be like pulling four of
your mates in a bathtub from
Edinburgh to London and back in the
freezing cold.

The straps creaked. Bit by bit they inched forward. It was possible – just.

At last they were on their way. To begin with, the weather was good; the only problem was a broken flask. The worst thing was pulling those heavy sledges day after day. Sometimes the thought of pulling them a few more metres was bad enough. The fact they had to haul them across the Antarctic began to make them angry and depressed.

Fact Box A

Facts about Antarctica

Forty million (40,000,000) years ago Antarctica was covered in trees.

Twenty million (20,000,000) years ago there was extensive ice.

Twelve million (12,000,000) years ago the great ice sheet had started to form.

The poles are so cold due to the low angle of the sun which means they get about 40% less sun than the equator.

After a while, Ranulph came to think of his sledge as a horrible monster that needed slaying. That thought kept him going every time his skis slid backwards on the ice.

Almost immediately, the harness straps began digging into their hips like sharp knives and the stiff waistbands rubbed their skin raw. Soon, Ranulph twisted his shoulder blades. But the pain was easy compared to the boredom. That really drove them crazy. Have you ever spent a day staring at nothing but your bedroom carpet? Imagine then, weeks staring at nothing except snow and ice.

They agreed to share the navigation. It's very hard *always* following! When you lead, you're busy working out the best route across the ice using the compass. You're scanning the land, sizing up problems the whole time. You've got something to do. Something to think about. When you're following there's nothing to do. Nothing to think about. And it drives you mad.

They swapped over the lead position every so often. Ranulph (who was always used to being the leader) got more and more annoyed every time it was Mike's turn to be in front. Mike was fitter,

*The gap between Fiennes and Stroud
– the cause of much friction – grows
ever bigger*

smaller, and eleven years younger, so he always covered more distance when he was out in front.

This led to problems. Ranulph said Mike was going too fast. He was wasting energy and using too many calories. They only had so much food to last the journey. They couldn't afford to lose too much weight. But Mike enjoyed pushing himself. He hated plodding along behind, especially when Ranulph changed track and Mike couldn't see a reason for it.

Blinding Ice

There you are, on blinding white ice. Nothing but this bent figure in front of you, and every time he sneezes, sniffs, or scratches his knee, the sound is magnified a thousand times. After a while, you want to yell at him to shut up.

This is a common problem on small expeditions, blaming your companion for everything. There isn't anyone else to get cross with. Think of spending week after week with just one person.

An explorer on Scott's famous Antarctic expedition said the loss of one biscuit crumb led to a mood which lasted a week. But knowing that didn't

always help Ranulph and Mike stay
friends.

One day, Mike was leading when
Ranulph fell up to his armpits into a
crevasse. Luckily the sledge harness held
him and he was able to get out while
Mike soldiered on. He didn't even know
Ranulph had fallen until he told
him about it later.

A climber carefully negotiates a deep crevasse, with the use of an aluminium ladder

They skied in a **white-out**, trying to avoid gaping crevasses, some wider than a motorway. New snow masked the edges of the crevasses and they couldn't see where a drop started or ended, making it even more dangerous than usual. In these conditions all they could do was go extra slowly, carefully. And hope their luck didn't give out.

Weak **snow bridges** covered the crevasses here and there and they couldn't tell if these narrow bridges would hold the weight of the sledges until they stepped on them. One bad move and down you go. That's it. The end.

Mike was going along carefully, when a man-sized crevasse suddenly opened up. Snow crashed and boomed from under him and down he went, up to his head.

Ranulph heard him
yelling and turned around.
If he hadn't, that would have been the
end of Mike and the end of their
crossing of Antarctica. Poor Mike was
stuck in no man's land, hanging over a
massive drop. Thankfully, his sledge had
caught half-way over the crevasse as he
fell. But if he moved a millimetre... he
would drop to his death, bringing the
sledge with him.

Quickly, Ranulph dropped his harness and grabbed the back of Mike's swinging sledge. He held it tight. And bit by bit, for the worst, few minutes of Mike's life, he carefully edged his way up the crevasse without once looking down. Between them, they pulled and pushed the sledge, until the whole thing was on solid ground again. The effort made Mike feel sick. Ranulph said his face at the end was the colour of beetroot.

When they set up the tent for the night, they could hear a storm raging outside. The ice was sighing and groaning as it always does on its constant move towards the sea. At any moment, a rumbling mass of ice could break away under them and take them with it, and no one would know how they died. Their bodies would be locked forever in their deep, icy beds.

Fact Box B

The sledges carried:
51 food bags
31 (1 litre) fuel bottles
Skis and sticks
Tent, poles, stakes and bag
Sleeping bags
2 cookers plus boxes and spare parts
2 mugs, 2 spoons, 2 pots, windproof matches
Windsail
Rope
Ice screws and axes
Snow shovels
Pee bottle
Medical kit
2 radio batteries
Beacons
Science kit
Sony video camera, 9 tapes and 2 batteries
Olympus 2000 camera and 10 films
2 Thermos flasks
Ski boots
Sledge jackets

A personal bag with all those little things that might come in handy:

needles, thimble, cord, wire, spanner, lighter, flints, screws, pencil, diary, superglue, chart, map, compass, army knife, goggles, socks.

Mike was very tired that night, light-headed and woozy. Suddenly the tent seemed too thin to keep out the raging storm. They hardly slept a wink and there was nothing to look forward to the next day but more crevasses, more freezing cold and more dragging those heavy sledges.

Next morning, Mike could hardly open the tent flap. He twiddled and twiddled, his cold fingers as clumsy as hammers. When at last he looked out, the sight was shocking.

There was nothing to see but a thick sheet of blinding white snow.

CHAPTER

3

That Little Jag of Ice

When the wind and snow cleared, Mike was shocked to see the pale blue light of a new crevasse only three steps in front of the tent. If they'd camped a metre away last night, the tent would have fallen in while they slept.

Setting out four hours late, they needed to make up the lost time so they attached the sails to the sledges for the first time. For a while it was fantastic, soaring over ice ridges, flying along.

When Mike heard Ranulph yell from up front he was going too fast to stop. Ranulph shouted again, trying to warn Mike of danger. At that very moment, Mike also spotted the problem ahead.

Too late to stop, Mike sailed into thin air, his sledge thudding into him from behind. Wind whistled past his face, time slowed to nothing and an eerie silence crowded in.

Ranulph began shouting, wondering where Mike had gone, but Mike was too stunned to answer. He'd landed on a ledge a few metres down and was stranded on a jag of ice, hanging over a deathly drop. Mike's sledge had jammed into the ice wall beyond, just missing his head. If it hadn't been for that little jag of ice...

Bit by bit Mike undid the sledge harness and began climbing to a safer ramp of snow.

At any moment, the ridge he was breathlessly climbing could break off, leaving him to slide down into the bottomless pit. Mike heard his own heartbeat echo around him, while he focused every brain cell on his next move.

Then Ranulph threw a rope and pulled up the contents of the sledge, item by item. They couldn't afford to

lose a single thing! Ranulph hauled up
the broken sledge and lastly, helped
Mike up. They had to spend hours
mending the sledge by drilling the parts
together again.

Fact Box C

Inside the food boxes were packs of:

Sugar
Butter
Tea
Cocoa
Chocolate
Dried milk
Corn oil
Oatmeal
Soup

Dried meats
Freeze dried meals
Freeze dried veg.
Bacon bars
Flapjack bars
Biscuits
Cereal
Raisins

That night, it was midnight before they camped and they hit another problem which could have ended the trip. The cooker was leaking. It was impossible to attach the fuel bottle. They knew they didn't stand a chance without a cooker. They needed it to melt snow and boil water, as well as heat food and warm their toes. Both men became jumpy and irritable when Ranulph unpacked the spare cooker and still couldn't attach the fuel bottle. For a while, everything seemed hopeless.

They didn't give up, though. They couldn't give up, so Mike set to work using some spare, plastic washers, which he cut down with nail scissors. He tried again and again to fix the leak. Having bodged something together, he lit a match and held his breath, hoping they wouldn't be blown to the South Pole.

It worked.

Hairy Soup

When the sky was clear, the sun burned down and they stripped down to their underwear. Soon they began suffering from that horrible itching that happens when you haven't washed for days. They threw away their warm duvet jackets to off-load some weight. This was something they'd regret later on, when **sixty-knot** winds blew into every pore and nipped their blisters.

Day 8

By the eighth day, they were suffering from soggy, blistery feet, aching limbs and sores where their clothes chafed their skin.

One morning, Ranulph woke up with his lips stuck together from sunburn. Picking and carefully tweaking, he very slowly prised them apart. Due to the hole in the **ozone layer**, the **ultra violet rays** from the sun touch the skin like red-hot flames. With only a few sun creams to last the trip, they had to use them sparingly. When Ranulph sat down to eat his porridge it was often spattered – not with raspberry juice, but blood. Yerk!

Soon, little problems blew up into

something bigger. Ranulph had a bad habit of clipping his beard and eyebrows in the middle of the tent. Mike kept finding hairs in his clothes, boots and worst of all, his soup! They had a discussion about it and finally, Ranulph agreed to do his clipping between his knees into a bag.

Ranulph started complaining about Mike racing ahead. And again, Mike didn't listen, said he was making a fuss about nothing. Each day, a tense competition built up between them.

Part of Mike's job on the expedition was to take samples of blood and urine

for testing when they got back. Every night they had to get up and use the urine bottle a couple of times. Mike needed to measure the urine output and take samples.

Also, every ten days, Mike had to take some of Ranulph's blood. Unfortunately, Ranulph was one of those people who hate needles and behaved as if Mike was his torturer. Sometimes it was difficult to find a vein. Now and then the blood wouldn't flow up the needle in the freezing cold. It was a real nightmare for Ranulph and one that got worse as time went on.

At times, they each secretly wished the other would give up, so they could call the whole thing off and go home. Of course, neither wanted to be the first to give in, so on they plodded.

One day there was such a terrible snowstorm outside, they were stuck in

the tent all day. There was little to do apart from mend bits of equipment. Ranulph made a lip mask out of elastic from his underwear. With a felt tip pen, Mike marked out a chess board on top

The explorers could regain their
composure once another day of
walking was over. Once in the tent,
they could unwind and relax a bit.
Despite harsh conditions, the two could
behave like the friends that they were

of the cooker box. They used the tubes of urine as chess pieces. Mike marked the tops: red for him, blue for Ranulph. It worked quite well. The full tubes, were of course, the kings and queens. Mike taught Ranulph how to play and he learnt quickly. It kept them happy all day.

Although out on the ice they sometimes behaved like bitter enemies, as soon as they entered the tent, everything was forgotten and they were friends again.

More Problems!

Going uphill was the worst. Often, the sledges dragged them back more steps than they managed to take. Sometimes they went slower than snails. Mike started to notice how thin and weedy he was getting, how bony he felt in his sleeping bag. And they weren't even half way yet.

Sir Ranulph pracising pulling a loaded sledge up an icefall during training in the Alps

Day 25

After twenty-five days they were both so tired, they dreamed of giving up. There was only a slim chance of success now. They had to get to the Ross Sea to reach the *Seaquest* ship before its departure date. The ship couldn't wait because the weather and sea conditions wouldn't be safe after that date.

Climbing the **sastrugi** wore them out the most – day after day of hauling sledges up ridges and sliding, falling, tripping down the other side. Then, at the end of all that hard work, there was nothing to look forward to but another stretch of sastrugi more awful than the last. Half the time the sledges slammed into their backs and occasionally they locked into a ridge just as they were being hauled over the top. Each of them messed up lots of times, getting skis caught, or something worse. Then

*Mike Stroud pulls his sledge
up one more time!*

they'd mutter under their breath.

Such awful, thankless work! Now Mike was suffering from a swollen abscess on his foot and taking **antibiotics**. Every time there was any pressure on the abscess, he was in agony. This, with the usual sores, aching shoulders and hips, made each day feel harder than the last.

They cheered up for a minute or two when they reached the 82nd **line of latitude** and celebrated with a king size chocolate bar. It tasted like heaven.

Mike turned his mind to the toy house he was going to build for his children when he got home. He planned every detail, over and over again. It was a good way of keeping his mind off his abscess and the weeks ahead.

But soon things got even worse. Mike got a stomach bug and three times he had to get up in the middle of the night.

In the morning, he managed to get going, even though he felt weak and dizzy.

They set off, and although Mike tried his best, he didn't last long. After about forty minutes, he was too sick to take another step.

Ranulph was furious with him. They'd only just started out and had no days

to lose. Mike took some tablets, drank some hot tea and slept for over four hours. Boy, did he need that sleep! Ranulph worked out a whole plot for a novel while Mike snored away.

Later they tried again, but Mike had to give up after a couple of hours. Ranulph was angry with him for cutting short the day. They were behind schedule and he blamed Mike for racing ahead earlier, and not saving energy.

Then Mike found his watch wasn't working. Ranulph had suggested that Mike have the battery checked before they set out for Antarctica, but Mike had been too busy to send it away. With only one watch between them they were in trouble as Mike needed a watch to navigate. This time, Ranulph was seething. In the end, he lent Mike *his* watch and told him to say when it was time to change over, every hour.

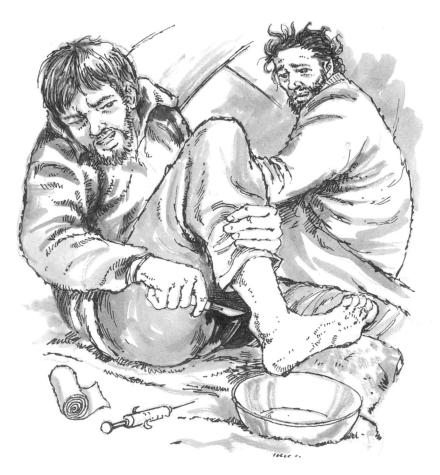

Mike spent that evening cutting his abscess. Once bandaged, he felt better than he had for days. Better than his partner, because by now Ranulph had nine, separate bandages on his feet.

Some of the plasters were stuck so hard he had to cut them off, bit by bit.

Things were getting so bad that both men had stopped caring about the future.

Keeping Going

When they set out the following morning, there was a **force eight** wind. It was horribly cold. Too cold to stop for their usual hot swigs from the flask. Normally, these little breaks kept them going. They broke up the day and gave them something to look forward to.

Sir Ranulph finds himself in a crevasse after sailing over the edge

They tried sailing. But the wind blew them straight into ice ridges, which ripped them to bits. By now, they couldn't bear any more injuries. In the end, they gave up and folded and bagged up the sails.

Mike was still suffering from a weak stomach and Ranulph was feeling sick too. They were both in such bad shape all they could do was laugh about it. The snow was fresh and soft. It was hard going to move very far at all. The **sledge runners** kept sinking into the new snow and every step took a superhuman effort. It was a bit like trudging through thick mud.

Ranulph had made a face mask to protect his sunburnt skin and at one point his beard became matted to the mask. When he tried to untangle it, skin came away in his hands, leaving a bleeding raw patch on his chin. Soon it turned poisonous and began swelling. Almost out of antibiotics, Mike had to give him the last few.

It was so cold when they set up the tent that night, there were icicles on Ranulph's face!

By this time Ranulph was spending most evenings cutting his frozen **balaclava** from his beard with a tiny pair of penknife scissors. Not a pretty sight. At least he did it over a bowl and not the cooking stove. No hairy soup this time!

Day 34

After thirty-four days, they were half-way to the Pole. The thought of another day, let alone another month, wasn't a happy one.

They were supposed to do fourteen kilometres a day. And every time they fell behind, they used up food they couldn't spare. This was getting dangerous. Already thin, and eating fewer calories than they needed, at the end of each day they were starving. They were so hungry, they begin to think the other was cheating, and eating more than their fair share. They eyed each other carefully at every meal, just like five-year-olds!

Then they had to deal with days of white-outs which are terrifying. Everything is white and you can't see where you are. You lose your balance and can go half-mad. Explorers have

been known to walk straight into crevasses in this kind of weather.

After one bad white-out, Mike made the mistake of taking his goggles off for a couple of hours. He was fed up with stopping every few minutes to wipe the mist away, and he forgot about the dangers of not wearing goggles.

Mike paid for his mistake later by getting snow-blindness. There's nothing quite like the pain of snow-blindness. Every time you blink it feels as if your eyes are being pricked with hot needles. Sadly, he had no choice but to put up with the pain.

By now, both men were not only losing weight but losing muscle, too.

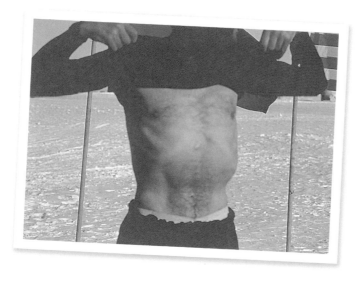

Ranulph Fiennes demonstrates his dramatic weight loss at the South Pole

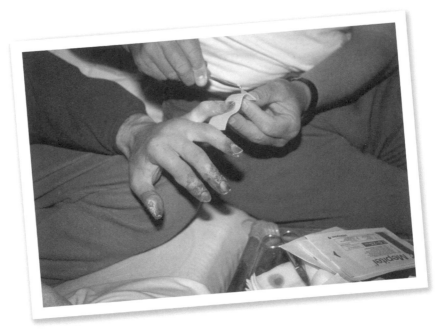

A doctor treats a climber's frostbitten hands

When the tests were done, Ranulph found he was using 10,000 calories per day and eating only 5,200. Some days, Mike said he could *feel* the weight falling off. By day fifty-one they'd both lost twenty per cent of their body weight.

Day 53

When Mike had another attack of sickness they had to stop after only two hours. Added to this, the temperature dropped and Mike became so cold he became woozy and unable to think clearly. He began to lose the feeling in his fingers and almost got severe **frost-bite**.

Their weeks of effort were beginning to tell.

CHAPTER

More Dead Than Alive

After sixty-eight days, they reached the South Pole, but they could not afford the time to rest. After spending two happy hours drinking tea and exchanging news with an American all-women team, they set out again. After that, things went downhill very quickly.

Days of force five, biting wind made them regret throwing away their warm duvet jackets earlier. With ice as hard as rock, it was hard to lift each blistered foot and frost-bitten finger and move at all.

Day 75

By the seventy-fifth day, Ranulph's feet were in such a mess that putting on his boots each morning felt like torture.

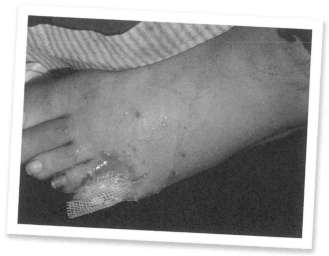

Frostbitten foot

Although he didn't want to take painkillers because they made him drowsy, Mike forced Ranulph to take a couple. Mike, though weak and starving, was mostly pain free.

When the **wind chill factor** fell to minus ninety degrees centigrade, it added to their physical problems. Now it was hard to breathe, let alone try to move. After losing his ski sticks when sailing his sledge, Mike had to borrow one from Ranulph and this slowed them down even more.

On half rations now, both men were near to collapse and skidded and slid down iron-hard ice, avoiding bottomless pits, as best they could. Hour after hour it was only luck that saved them from near death falls.

On the eighty-second day, Mike twisted his foot sailing on the wind. He struggled on with the pain. Much later,

Antarctica's vast Beardmore Glacier: at 260 miles (418 km) long, it is one of the world's biggest

he learned he'd cracked a bone in his ankle.

Day 86

When they crossed the Beardmore Glacier and reached the ice shelf they were at last on the final leg of the journey. But as they set up their ninetieth camp, on the eighty-sixth day since they set out, they checked their rations and found they only had food enough for nine more days.

They were still a long way from the *Seaquest* ship, which was due to leave in eight days time. They had to make a decision soon. Their only ski-plane was due to leave the area in four days! If the plane had to stay any longer than that, Ranulph would have to pay two thousand pounds per extra day.

They crossed part of the ice shelf in a white-out in order to reach a safer landing spot. After five more painful hours, Mike was so cold he became listless and was unable to speak without slurring his words. Ranulph had no choice but to set up the tent and quickly make tea and chocolate to bring Mike round. It was their final day of reckoning.

The blizzard season was due to begin and Ranulph, at last, suggested they give up.

Almost time to call it a day!

Day 95

Only when finally aboard the ski-plane did they realise how ill they were. They felt more dead than alive. The warmth of the plane made their limbs swell, made them feel giddy and unable to talk or sit up.

Was it worth it?

Well, after ninety-five days these brave men had covered 2,380 kilometres under the worst possible conditions. They went into the Guinness Book of Records as: *The longest totally self supporting polar sledge journey ever made and the first totally unsupported crossing of the Antarctic land mass were achieved by R. Fiennes and M. Stroud.*

They raised two million pounds for charity and were awarded the OBE.

Story Background

Fantastic Facts

❄ There are more than twelve species of whale in the Southern Ocean including: Blue whales, Minke whales, Humpback whales, Killer (Orca) Whales (shown in the picture below) and one called a Long Finned Pilot!

❄ The Antarctic food chain is dependent upon Krill which are the staple diet for most whales. Sadly, overfishing of Krill is destroying the **ecosystem**.

❄ There are dolphins, porpoises, and six kinds of seal. Including one called a Southern Elephant Seal.

❊ In the last fifty years some parts of Antarctica have warmed up by 2.5 degrees centigrade. If the Western ice sheet melts – the extra water could raise sea levels by 5-6 metres.

❊ On March 5th 2002 the Larsen Ice Shelf (3,250 sq km of ice) broke up and fell into the sea.

❊ Scientists from 27 countries work in the Antarctic. The picture below shows one of the research bases in Antarctica.

If you can bear the pain... find out more about their awful journey by reading *Mind Over Matter* by Ranulph Fiennes and *Shadows On The Wasteland* by Mike Stroud

Index

Glossary

antibiotics medicine to destroy bacteria

balaclava woollen covering for head and neck

crevasses deep open cracks in ice

ecosystem fine balance of nature and physical environment

force eight very high wind speed

frost-bite injury to the body due to freezing

line of latitude an imaginary line round the earth. 0 is the equator, 90 degrees N or S are the North and South Poles

ozone layer a layer in the stratosphere 50km above the earth's surface that absorbs most of the sun's harmful ultraviolet radiation

sastrugi sharp-ridged ice dunes

sixty-knot one knot is 1.85 km an hour

ski-plane a plane which has skis and can land on ice or snow

sledge runners the skis under a sledge which enable it to run on the snow and ice

snow-blind loss of eyesight due to the glare of the ice and snow, usually temporary

snow bridges areas of snow formed over crevasses which may look safe but are unstable

ultra violet rays rays from the sun. Can be harmful if skin unprotected

white-out a snowstorm which is so dense that it is not possible to see anything

wind chill factor when the temperature feels much colder because of the wind